W9-CRF-200

All

Is

One Life

All Is One Life

Golden Moments
of
Insight, Inspiration, and Awareness

BERT GERLITZ

BLUE DOLPHIN PUBLISHING

Published by
Blue Dolphin Publishing, Inc.
P.O. Box 8, Nevada City, CA 95959
Orders: 1-800-643-0765

ISBN: 1-57733-010-2

Library of Congress Cataloging-in-Publication Data

Gerlitz, Bert, 1926–
    All is one life : golden moments of insight,
  inspiration, and awareness / Bert Gerlitz.
        p.   cm.
    ISBN 1-57733-010-2 (hardcover)
    1. Life.   I. Title.
  BD435.G44   1998
  128—dc21   98-8839
                                                CIP

Cover art: Lito Castro

Printed in the United States of America

10   9   8   7   6   5   4   3   2   1

Contents

Introduction

The impetus for this book came about when one of my grandchildren asked some pertinent questions about the purpose of Life.

This made me realize that these are perennial questions confronting individuals of every age and generation.

I am now seventy years of age, and have also sought for explanations concerning our relationship to nature and the cosmos; the real meaning of Life; and the cycle of birth and death.

During my lifetime, my search gained considerable motivation by studying various teachings, disciplines, and philosophies. However, I felt that I had looked at concepts and beliefs without seriously delving inside myself for confirmation. And, thus, I had yet to achieve the deep understanding I was seeking. Consequently, I decided to rely on the benefit of quiet contemplation in order to find the vital links that had eluded me.

On numerous walks, surrounded by nature in the great outdoors, I observed and pondered. My anchor, guide and inspiration was divine Life within and around me.

Subsequently, I gained profound insights concerning interrelatedness of existence. And, I perceived that All Is One Life—the One Divine Life.

This volume is dedicated to those who cherish their connectedness with the totality of Life and feel keenly about nature and the global environment.

1

Serenity

Walking through a meadow and forest, I was more than ever conscious of the abundant Life around me.

The grass, the wildflowers, the majestic conifers, the stately maples, the lacy ferns, the many species of birds, the deer, the insects, the lizards, the sun, the clouds, and the cascading stream, were just some of the evidence of Life which I witnessed.

I became very quiet as I contemplated the interconnection of everything I saw, and thought of the many questions about Life which had perplexed me in the past.

At this point, I joyfully realized that my search for clues for these puzzling questions was over. Insights gained by previous meaningful experiences with Life, through nature, provided the answers I had sought.

The first of several important events occurred, unexpectedly, in a blossom-filled orchard, and was followed by many others in a variety of settings.

Successively, these experiences confirmed and solidified my inner perception about the oneness of Life, and provided the individual threads which resulted in making up the fabric of my understanding and awareness of Life's reality.

2

The Orchard

It was on a balmy spring morning that I found myself in an apricot orchard in Northern California.

The trees were covered with pink blossoms. The bees were buzzing. I stood in awe of all the beauty around me.

A most thought-provoking thing happened to me at that time.

As I stood in this tranquil orchard, I was oblivious to everything except the sun, the trees, the bees, and myself.

I became very cognizant of shadows.

Specifically, my attention was riveted by the shadows of the rows of trees. I turned around, and I also saw my own shadow clearly on the ground. Simultaneously, I observed the miniature shadows of the bees at the blossoms.

Seeing the individual shadows, under these special circumstances, acted as a catalyst to a new comprehension for me.

Instantly, this thought flashed in my mind, "There are not three entities here, completely separate of each other. This very moment, the trees, the bees, and I are one Life—there is connectedness."

I rested in the realization of a oneness that was beautifully revealing.

It was a very calm, and unforgettable, moment that expanded my awareness of Life, immeasurably.

3

The View from the Mountain Top

I was on a wintertime hike in the mountains. There was snow on the ground, and it was quite cold and cloudy.

As I reached the mountain top, I saw the valley below including a lake surrounded by numerous trees. I paused, momentarily, to admire the beautiful view.

Without any warning, except for the cold temperature, it started to hail.

I looked to the valley and saw snow falling in several lower-elevation areas. Further down, it was raining, and around the lake I could see a fine mist rising. Observing this panorama, I also noticed my warm exhaled breath, like a miniature mist, merging with the cold air around me.

It was at that point that the following thought surfaced: "Things appear to be different, but they are really, in essence, one. Yes, the hail, the snow, the rain, the mist, the water in the lake, the water in the cells of the trees, and the water in the cells of my own body, all interrelate."

I recognized the water, which I saw simultaneously in its various forms, to be an integral part of the one Life. Therefore, I was once again left with the awareness that, while form is varied and diverse, the substance remains identical.

4

Among the Stars

Never had I seen the stars as brilliant as that night on a Polynesian island.

What made it so memorable for me was that I saw stars both above and below.

Standing on a bluff overlooking a mirror-smooth lagoon, fringed by palm trees, I could also see the stars reflected in crystal sharpness.

The sight of the stellar abundance, its luminescence, and magnitude, made me truly feel that I was among the stars—which, in reality, I was—and not just looking at them.

I allowed my mind to briefly wander, and imagined what it would be like to live on an island in complete concert with all of life.

Under this scenario, I visualized there would surely be:

Absolute reliance on the island's ecological self-sufficiency in the absence of malls, supermarkets, freeways, and fast food outlets.

Recognition of the island's certain decline if there were abuse, permanent reduction, or destruction of its resources.

Appreciation that the streams, the ocean, the fish, the coconut palms, and other flora and fauna are symbiotic necessities of Life.

A genuine feeling of custodianship for the island and its environment.

I gazed at the stars for a very long time while with every cell and fiber of my being I fully appreciated the magnificence of this planet, this galaxy, and this very existence.

5

Watching the Sunset

With my dog "Shep" at my side, I went to the horse corral, in back of the barn, to saddle up "Flex" for a ride up the hill.

As I reached to take my horse's saddle off the rack, I decided to ride him bareback instead.

I knew that Flex preferred to not have the warm blanket and a cinched-up saddle at the end of a hot summer's day.

After putting the bridle on Flex, I grabbed his long mane and swung myself on his back.

And off we were, the three of us.

We left the pastures, with grazing cows, and were soon among large oak trees covered with maturing acorns.

Steadily climbing in elevation, we came to a zone supporting madrones and manzanita, and traversed an area of chaparral broom and sagebrush. We ultimately arrived at the mountain ridge where the grass was interspersed with lupines.

By now, the sun was fairly low and the heat of the day had dissipated. I sensed that both Flex and Shep enjoyed the freedom of this unconfined spot as much as I did.

We rested for a few minutes upon arriving at the top of the ridge. From up here, one could see the Pacific Ocean, some eleven miles to the west.

It took almost no prompting on my part to have Flex gallop, exuberantly, along the ridge toward the setting sun. This continued for nearly a third of a mile, with Shep following us at his own pace.

We reached the end of the ridge just as the sun was dipping below the horizon.

Shep had caught up with us by now, and all three of us were quietly facing the setting sun. Three pairs of eyes reflected those golden rays and the afterglow that followed.

I lost all track of time while watching the sunset in close association with my companions, and feeling completely united in the Life that we shared.

We remained a long time on top of the mountain, before finally winding our way back down by the light of the moon.

6

The Meadow

A preferred hiking destination for me is a meadow above the village.

The traffic noise and other sounds from the valley first dim and then disappear entirely, as I approach this large, grassy area.

I have enjoyed the peace and quiet of this spot many times. However, on a particular late summer morning, I had a unique and mind-stimulating experience.

When I reached the meadow, I proceeded to walk along the trail that cuts diagonally across it.

The wild grass was dry, and each waist-high stalk was topped by a ripe seedhead.

I remembered it was only a few months earlier that this same meadow was lush and velvety green. Each slender blade of grass was, then, just poking its tip out of the moist ground.

As I arrived at the center of the meadow, a mild breeze came up. I was looking across a sea of seedheads gently swaying in unison. That was when it happened.

All at once, I no longer saw dry grass topped by ripe seedheads. Instead, I saw Life expressing through what appeared as millions of individual, intelligent, manifestations experiencing youth to maturity.

At that moment, I sensed a strong parallel and bond between the Life of each stalk of grass and my own Life.

On my walk back to the village, I contemplated the significance of what I had just seen and sensed.

Having recognized the connectedness of the grass with Life's oneness, I knew that, from that day forward, I would look at a meadow from a different perspective.

7

The Dragonflies

Rounding the path, I was quickly encircled by about twenty dragonflies.

They were actively involved in their acrobatics, flitting here and there. I was entranced, and watched their every maneuver.

In their infancy, these dragonflies spent months on end as nymphs crawling in the slimy and muddy bottom of streams and ponds. They were busy feeding on all kinds of aquatic larvae and insects.

Now, they were gracefully soaring under the open sky with their delicate, colorful, wings. This transition is another stunning example of Life's vitality, intelligence, and certainty of purpose.

There was not the slightest hint of their prior state of existence as crawling nymphs—they were glorious expressions of Life in the present moment. My involvement, through my observation and awareness, made me conscious of the importance of being in this ever-present now.

The dragonflies clearly exemplified for me that Life creates conditions that are transitory. These changing conditions reflect the dynamic energy of Life. Not change for the sake of change, but change as an integral process of Life.

The short chance encounter with the dragonflies left me with renewed appreciation of Life's ongoing course of transformation.

8

On the Trail to the Epicenter

Several years after California's devastating Loma Prieta earthquake in 1989, I drove to the forest which was the location of that quake's epicenter.

I entered the lush forest area—my destination for the day.

After parking the car, I hiked through the densely wooded terrain accompanied, at each step, by the sound of a rushing stream.

Ferns were waist-high along the trail

and on the river banks, and there was a profusion of periwinkle with dark green leaves and lavender-blue flowers. Emerald green moss was everywhere, especially on rocks and tree trunks.

It did not take me very long to forget the hustle and bustle of the outside world.

The forest is a few miles inland from the Pacific Ocean, yet, I noticed considerable sediments from the sea in the cliffs about eight feet above the trail. In addition, there was a deposit of highly polished smooth gravel from what must have been an ancient beach exposed to pounding waves, eons ago.

Many, many years ago the ocean had been where I was now strolling under trees.

I stopped, abruptly, when I heard crashing noises in the thicket ahead. I knew that this sound was definitely not that of deer.

The suspense did not last too long before the roamers revealed themselves.

It was a family consisting of a huge wild boar and a sow, with several piglets in tow. They paraded right in front of me without being aware of my presence. However, they soon sauntered off, leaving as quickly as they had appeared.

About ten minutes later along the trail, I became engrossed in watching the behavior of a colony of small, winged, insects which had made their home in a cliff of soft sandstone.

I noticed they were flying in from all directions, evidently returning from foraging expeditions. As some of the insects were either entering or leaving their abode's opening, I observed others in a "holding pattern" awaiting their turn for ingress.

In the activities I observed, the insects were exhibiting characteristics which were not exclusive to their species. It was fascinating, for instance, to see Life's intelligence, coupled with memory, in use to promote the colony's survival. It was equally fascinating to realize, again, that all manifestations of Life possess the same basic attributes for this purpose.

Observing the innate intelligence and sense of

order of these insects reinforced my awareness of Life's oneness and connectedness.

To reach the epicenter, I then followed a winding trail which sometimes hugged the side of a hill and, occasionally, dipped down so that one could cross a number of creeks.

Since I was wearing sandals that day, it was relatively easy to remove them while crossing the streams. Walking on the sandy and gravelly bottom, while the cool, refreshing water massaged my feet, was a delight to the senses.

Along the trail, I noticed that some of the wider sections were, at one time, part of a long-gone logging operation. The tell-tale signs were the many short sections of logs embedded close together across the trail. The cut trees could then be pulled by horses or mules with greater ease.

There was also evidence of a large ramp, constructed of logs, which had facilitated sending the cut trees to the stream below. From there, they could be floated to a milling operation downstream. Those early pioneers were certainly an ingenious lot.

The trail was quiet and peaceful. The only sounds were the stream, my own footsteps, and the occasional croaking of frogs, chattering of squirrels, and the drilling of woodpeckers.

As I rounded a bend in the trail, I immediately knew that I had arrived at my destination.

The whole hillside was covered with uprooted trees. Slides and ground-shifting were apparent everywhere.

I knew that this was the epicenter even before seeing an official marker just off the trail. The marker bore the inscription:

Epicenter

10/17/89

7.1 Magnitude

Latitude 37.03°N

Longitude 121.88°W

My mind went back to the time of the earthquake.

When the quake struck, I was on the sixth floor of an office building. Having gone through a number of preparedness drills, I instinctively dove under the closest desk. With my legs pulled up under my arms, I felt like a pretzel in this confined space.

I could sense the whole building swaying as I sat tightly squeezed in my little cubbyhole. I did not know what the outcome would be.

It seemed like an eternity, but it was actually only a brief time until the temblors subsided. Everyone on that floor decided to quickly evacuate by taking the steps down to the street.

As soon as I could, I tried to telephone home to find out if everything was all right. I guess a lot of other people in the area had the same idea to call their home. It took some time, therefore, before my call went through. Fortunately, my wife was unharmed.

Listening to the news, later, we found out that this quake had caused much havoc and devastation in the region.

All this went through my mind as I stood at that quake's epicenter at what was now a peaceful and serene moment in this forest.

And I pondered on this penetrating question which I posed to myself:

"How do major natural phenomena such as earthquakes, volcanoes, tidal waves, hurricanes, floods, and tornadoes relate to the many and varied manifestations of Life, including myself?"

I stayed in deep contemplation at the epicenter site for about another twenty minutes, before heading back and retracing my steps along the trail.

Entering a sunlit spot on the path, I was cognizant of a spider web suspended under the lowest branch of an old oak tree. An approximately eight-foot long strand produced by the spider was holding its web securely in place.

With the sun behind, the web and strands were transformed into a kaleidoscope of color. Blue predominated, and purple, orange, yellow, red, and green, all contributed to an overall magical effect. What a truly beautiful sight. And, to complete nature's artistry, the sun backlighted hundreds of tiny insects whose delicate, translucent, silvery wings were shimmering in the evening sunlight, nearby.

After this unexpected interlude, I continued my walk back to the car, still pondering the earlier question pertaining to quakes and other major natural phenomena.

Soon I realized intuitively:

Whether gentle or cataclysmic, every manifestation is an integral, connected part of the one Life—never a separate event.

Life is in continuous creation—from spider webs to stars.

I can now relate to major natural phenomena in a totally different light and dimension.

9

The Tidepool

I was spending a day at California's Point Lobos which has been called "the greatest meeting of land and water in the world."

Seagulls and pelicans patrolled the coast. I watched their comings and goings while sitting adjacent to a tidepool at the ocean's edge. Offshore, I saw sea lions basking in the sun.

Before long, I lowered my gaze to the tidepool which was about twenty-five feet in diameter.

It was captivating to see the abundance of forms of Life in this microcosm which was being, periodically, replenished with a new supply of mineral-rich ocean water. This looked like a separate little world, but it was a wonderfully important part of Life's totality.

The crabs, starfish, anemones, and a myriad of other creatures, along with sea vegetation, were all living their individual lives. And, yet, all were invisibly and symbiotically linked to one another and to all of Life, beyond.

For a fleeting moment my mind wandered from the tidepool to me, a human being; to all of humanity; to the other forms of Life; and finally, to the Sun, the Moon, and to the distant stars.

The mind's journey took seconds, but that moment bridged for me the microcosm with the macrocosm. I recognized that Life has no limits.

The Forest

Occasionally, I would walk in a particular forest of majestic conifers. I would, then, also see deer and squirrels, and almost always there were numerous jays perennially bringing the color of the sky to eye level with their blue plumage.

Once again entering this grove of trees, I paused and closed my eyes. I wanted to fully savor the fresh, invigorating, smell of this place.

I still had my eyes closed when I heard the melodious sounds of a nearby brook.

The smell and sounds of the forest transmitted messages of welcome to my senses. I was truly glad to be there.

Upon opening and lifting my eyes, I noticed the tree tops swaying rhythmically back and forth in the wind.

Absorbing the atmosphere of the forest prepared me for further experiences.

Strolling along, I soon left the sounds of the brook behind.

I was enjoying the powerful silence of the forest when, intuitively, I recognized that the trees and I are expressions of one Life.

I comprehended that there were not really "trees" surrounding a "man" on this little spot of this particular planet, at this moment in time, but one Life manifesting differently.

This realization of all-inclusive oneness produced a now familiar wave of calmness within me.

I continued my forest walk serenely, looking at

the "trees" and at "myself" with a deep and significant awareness of Life.

11

The Rock at the Beach

I was leisurely walking along the beach after what seemed like an endless series of storms. Almost one month of pounding waves had severely transformed this normally smooth stretch of sand.

Driftwood of all sizes and descriptions was piled into a practically solid wall about four feet high and close to a half mile long.

Instead of smooth sand, there was a countless number of rocks ranging from immense boulders to tiny pebbles. All of these had been uncovered by the relentless force of the waves.

As I strolled and glanced around, my attention was attracted to a small, brownish-colored rock with what appeared to be a white marbled pattern.

The rock was about three inches long, two inches wide, and about three quarters of an inch thick. I decided to pick it up and study it.

I noticed, to my surprise and amazement, that this was no ordinary rock, but a marvelous fossil preservation.

What gave the "rock" the marbled effect were many small white sea shells firmly embedded in its body. By examining it closely I could see the intricate details of individual shells.

It was quite obvious that what I held in my hand was not just a rock, but a time capsule from long ago. It was once grit and ooze of an ancient sea which, under hydrostatic pressure, locked in and preserved the shells.

I began to realize that eons ago intelligent Life had produced these shells from what was then Life's symbiotic environment. Life then, as now, knew exactly what to do and how to do it in order to fulfill Life's constant manifestation.

The fossil shells that were now in my hand contained the evidence of the basic elements that went into producing them such as: the sun's heat, the water, and the minerals.

Here, millenniums after Life manifested as shells, I am a manifestation of that same Life—a Life that effectively bridges time without pause.

While reflecting on the wonders of Life, I looked further at the "rock" to see what else I could learn.

The "rock" itself was hard and solid. My mind probed at its origin. Before being a "rock" were its components not also mud, sand, lava and magma at times—and, way back, interstellar galactic particles? The "rock" contained the elements of cosmic existence. Wow!

I felt the infinity and interrelation of all of Life. The very ongoing Life of which I am an integral part.

I could not help but to hold the "rock" ever so tightly and reverently in my hand.

12

The Ring of Trees

California coast redwoods can live to an approximate age of two thousand years and reach a height of more than two hundred feet.

When these giants fall, either by an act of nature or by human hand, new trees sprout in the area of the original tree's base.

I was standing in the center of such a ring of redwoods. This circle had a circumference of about eighty feet.

The mother tree was long gone.

There was no trace of it to be seen nor a clue as to the cause of its demise.

I counted a total of twenty-five stately redwoods which now reached toward the sky and provided a sheltering canopy nearly one hundred and fifty feet above the ground.

In the silence of the moment I suddenly heard steps approaching. I glanced to the edge of the circle. Spotlighted in a shaft of sunlight stood a deer. It had discovered a supply of ripe plums which had dropped from a wild plum tree growing on the circle's perimeter.

For quite a while I remained undetected by the browsing deer, as I stood motionless and observing.

Contemplating this tranquil scene I lost all sense of time, separateness and self. Instead, I once again felt a complete harmony and connection.

Instinctively, I knew that there was one Life, breathing and manifesting in the forms of redwoods, plum tree, deer, and human being.

It was a beautiful feeling of oneness that was engendered in my consciousness.

13

Snorkeling in the Virgin Islands

One day, while in the US Virgin Islands, I donned snorkel, mask, and fins and made my way out to the reef area.

Gliding through the water, I was amazed by the multicolored and multibranched coral below me. There were many different types of coral, varying in shape, size, structure, and hue.

Coral is all the more precious when one considers that it grows at an extremely slow rate. It takes millions of polyps to build these fragile coral reefs.

I also watched with much interest the great variety of tropical fish darting about. They were distinguished by diverse shapes, sizes, hues, and idiosyncrasies. All were beautifully illuminated by the filtered rays of the sun.

In addition to the forests of coral and the many fishes in this grand marine setting, I also saw a wonderful array of sponges, lobsters, urchins, anemones, moon jellies, and even giant sea turtles.

It was in this placid setting that I was completely absorbed in studying the details of my surroundings, through the glass of my mask.

Abruptly, I found myself in the midst of a school of fish, numbering in the thousands, which were exploring their neighborhood.

It was a unique sensation for me. I had, of course, many times, been in crowds with thousands of fellow human beings. However, now I was moving along with this aquatic multitude.

For a brief period, I continued quite aware of

myself and the school of fish as separate entities sharing space in the water.

Suddenly, the demarcation of separateness disappeared, and I no longer saw them as "fish." There was no longer a feeling of "I" and "they." I was conscious only of being part of a breathing, pulsating, all encompassing oneness.

Later, as I swam back to shore, this consciousness expanded to include the sky and all the flora and fauna of this lovely island.

14

Encounter
with an Iris

The clump of wild iris under the madrone tree was blooming again.

I admired its delicate flowers with finely veined petals. They were a splash of color in a shady spot.

I looked at these flowers in a special way, because I remembered standing in this very location the previous year, and appreciating them equally at that time. It made me wonder what the flowers experienced during their blooming period last year. I also wondered about this plant's lifespan.

Viewing the flowers again, in their full splendor, confirmed for me that their existence from bud to fading, year after year, is the ongoing manifestation of Life. Furthermore, I perceived no evidence of a lifespan in the iris. On the contrary, everything pointed to a Life without interruption.

Some day, this entire clump of iris will revert to the forest's humus. When that happens, there will be no termination, either. Because, what manifested as iris, before, remains a part of the ever-present cycle of Life.

I saw in the iris a demonstration of the continuity of Life.

Little did I anticipate how much was to be learned by pondering on this blooming iris under the madrone tree.

15

In the Midst of Endless Life

California's Big Sur coastline beckoned me, and so I arrived at this rugged and spectacularly beautiful location at about 9:30 AM. I was most anxious to spend many hours there savoring the changing experiences of the day.

The hillsides were covered with dense growth of Monterey pine and coast redwoods, thus creating a very dramatic backdrop to this coastal setting.

Because there was no road leading directly to the ocean, I had to park my car and hike in for a short distance. My knapsack contained some bottled water, sunscreen lotion, a peanut butter sandwich, and a beach towel.

I hiked along the edge of a slow moving stream which meandered through fertile grass land.

The willows which lined the banks of the stream provided shelter for a great variety of animals. In addition, there were countless birds including California quail. Coveys of these quail had their ever-present lookout positioned on one of the higher branches. Upon hearing the lookout's signal, the entire covey would take off in a whirr.

The sight of a grove of eucalyptus trees was reinforced by the fragrance of their leaves which was carried in my direction by the gentle ocean breeze.

The fast-growing eucalyptus was originally imported from Australia by the early settlers as a potential source of wood for fence posts. Since then, these trees have naturalized in many areas of the state.

Approaching the grove, I noticed something very unusual. These trees seemed to have quite colorful leaves moving rapidly. Besides, I could not understand how the gentle breeze could create such motion.

The mystery was solved as soon as I reached the base of the first tree.

I had, unwittingly, stumbled upon a haven for monarch butterflies. Each orange-brown butterfly had an approximately three to four inch wingspan. The wings were bordered in black, with white dots.

In tune with Life's intelligence, these colorful creatures migrate as much as one thousand miles, from as far away as Canada, to spend winters in this area. They follow the routes of previous generations.

It was hard to estimate how many thousands of monarchs made this grove an annual home. Each tree was covered from tip to bottom branches with this quivering manifestation superimposed over the leaves of their host.

It was soon after departing from the eucalyptus grove that I observed the maneuvers of a hummingbird. I first saw it sitting quietly at the end of a willow branch. Suddenly, it flew straight up with its red crown and throat feathers sparkling in the sunlight. Higher and higher it flew, about a hundred feet, until it was only a speck in the sky. Then, with meteoric velocity, it plummeted toward the ground only to repeat this performance again and again, several times in a row. At the bottom of each dive it would make a "clicking" kind of a sound, before ascending. I marveled at the vitality, intelligence, accuracy, and what seemed to be just pure joy of living in this tiny manifestation of Life.

As I proceeded, a medley of bird calls announced the location of a delta where the stream entered the Pacific Ocean.

Hundreds of seagulls, as well as many pelicans

and cormorants, swarmed around and swam in the water. Undoubtedly, they relished the morsels carried by the stream.

Before me stretched a beautiful, long, wide, sandy beach which I would get to know well that day.

For the initial one hundred yards, it was slow going, because of the large amount of kelp deposited on the sand. This kelp came from the many beds that flourish in the waters off the coast. An underwater canyon furnishes the cold, mineral-rich, water for this profusion of sea vegetation.

The kelp, brought in by the tide, was still wet and acted like a magnet for hordes of small, slow-moving flies.

As I gingerly picked my way through this mass of slippery seaweed, these flies found the perspiration on my forehead equally attractive. However, as soon as I got to the open sand again they disappeared, and I could continue, comfortably.

It was a glorious day with not a cloud in the sky to be seen anywhere. The light blue of the sky was blending with the dark blue of the ocean.

After walking along two thirds of the length of the beach, I moved over to the sand dunes and spread out my towel. This was a good spot to rest, take a dip in the ocean, and have lunch.

I sat down with my back supported by the contouring sand dune. This enabled me to have an unobstructed, one-hundred-and-eighty-degree view of the beach.

The waves were soothingly lapping the shore. Sandpipers were scurrying along, following the advancing and receding water. In the distance were the water plumes of a pod of migrating whales.

With such a serene setting, it was no wonder that I dozed off for a great forty-minute nap.

Upon awakening, I took a quick, refreshing dip in the ocean, and then ate my peanut butter sandwich with gusto.

It was time to explore further, and so I packed up and continued.

I had strolled along but a few minutes when I heard, and then spotted, a waterfall on a rock outcropping.

The temptation was too intense to resist. I was soon luxuriating in the waterfall's cool spray with the ocean in front of me. I finished up by leaning against the dry rock at the side of the fall. This rock was toasty-warm, having absorbed the direct heat of the sun.

While feeling the exhilaration of the moment, I wondered if, at this same time, each water molecule of the cascade also experienced exhilaration of Life.

As I was being supported by the rock, I happened to look up and noticed vigorous plants where the water plunged over the top. Looking closer, I recognized this to be wild watercress growing in abundance.

I made a mental note that, on the way back, I would climb up and further inspect the cress. I had many memories of how good watercress tasted in salads. It always made a delicious meal by fixing it with a dressing of olive oil and lemon juice.

For the time being, however, I wanted to go to the end of this beach and so I moved on.

I was back at the water's edge, when my day's quiet reverie was interrupted by discovering a dead pelican. I paused, and silently paid my respect to a fellow creature.

Thereafter, the thought about this dead pelican did not leave me during the walk to the end of the beach.

The question that kept surfacing in my mind was, "What is this condition that we customarily label 'death'?"

Step by step I thought about it, as I returned along the two-mile beach.

This thought activity stopped only momentarily while climbing up to look at the watercress thriving on top of the fall.

Step by step, I kept reflecting. By reliving the events and sights of the day, the answer slowly evolved. It was this. "The multifaceted Life that I had witnessed on that beautiful day provided over-whelming evidence of Life's endlessness."

Life goes on. I realized this was so true about every manifestation of Life around me. I knew it was true about the: trees, monarch butterflies, hummingbirds, seaweed, waterfall, ocean, whales, and the pelican that I had seen.

I had, previously, classified all these manifesta-tions separately. However, I now perceived they were not for one moment separate. I was conscious of the absolute oneness of Life linking the diversity of existence.

Likewise, the pelican at every stage of existence was a manifestation of the one, all-encompassing, endless Life. And the pelican's condition, when I found it on the beach, was but a phase in Life's continuity of expression.

At this point of my contemplation, I knew that, because the pelican was never separate from the oneness of Life, it's "death" was a misnomer.

I comprehended the "pelican" was Life, and Life does not die.

Undoubtedly, scavengers, worms, and bacteria would soon appear at the scene. With my new perception, I understood that they, too, are integral to the one indivisible Life which is constantly manifesting.

Intuitively, I realized what I had observed was not a dead pelican, but the transformation of dynamic Life.

The endlessness of Life was very real for me, that day.

16

The Moss
and the Fir Tree

It was the first sunny day after almost a week of constant rain, ranging from drizzles to downpours.

Hiking through an area of predominantly evergreen trees, I noticed the beneficial effect of the rain on the forest. The dust which had accumulated during the summer months was washed off, and the ground was saturated. This allowed the trees to breathe freely, and the roots to perform their task of transporting water and nutrients up their trunks.

59

I observed another thing, as well. The moss on the tree trunks looked luxurious and vigorous compared to its shriveled appearance during its dormancy in summer.

Seeing the moss on trees was not a new thing for me, but this time I looked intently, closely, and analytically. It was also the time that it occurred to me to make certain kinds of comparisons.

I decided to pick a single segment of moss from the mass that was covering the tree trunk.

When I examined the moss closely, I was utterly surprised and amazed that it looked like a tiny replica of the giant conifer, its host.

"A pure coincidence," I said to myself. I was ready to dismiss the matter and to be on my way. But there was something deep inside my being that told me to hold on, because the similarity was not really a coincidence at all.

Numerous pertinent thoughts and questions followed in rapid succession.

While holding the moss between my fingers, I thought that, except for size, the tree and the moss actually have a great deal in common. For instance, they both:

- need moisture, air, light, and nutrients
- possess inherent intelligence
- reproduce, to continue the species.

My thinking process continued, by extension, to other forms of life.

Thus, just as moss is distinct from, yet similar, in many ways, to a tree, so, for example, also do the following diverse creatures have certain characteristics in common: lizard, alligator, rabbit, kangaroo, cat, tiger, otter, shark, hummingbird, flamingo, mouse, elephant. The list is limitless.

However distinct, these species all share the same basic needs for their existence. Observation reveals a definite unity in what appears as diversity.

What, then, accounts for the great discrepancy in size and appearance?

From moss to elephant—I had started on a journey from which there was now no turning back.

Species have been classified by the volumes, and even more remain to be identified.

The task I had set for myself was to comprehend the common element.

In previous academic studies, I had learned to identify by name over one thousand plants of all kinds. I accomplished this by noting their differences. Now, I was seeking the one unifying constituent.

Was this task achievable or too monumental?

The questions as to the source of all that is, and what accounts for the great variations, dominated my mind.

I decided to forge ahead and to rely, totally, on that which every being possesses. I knew that intuitive guidance would, ultimately, provide the sought for answers.

With the questions in my head, and the moss

in my hand, I left the forest. I would return the next day to continue my contemplation.

At home that evening, I studied the tree-like moss under a high-powered magnifying instrument. Seeing the beautiful detail made me more determined than ever to pursue the elusive answer to the question: what accounts for similarities as well as differences of all that is?

Early the next morning saw me continue the previous day's quest. I was confident that intuitive clarity would prevail.

I headed again for the moss-covered trees where I could commune with nature about the reality of Life.

Being immersed in nature, I felt one with my surroundings.

I returned to the same spot three days in a row.

Toward the end of the third day of concentrated contemplation, I apprehended Life manifests similarly, or differently, according to prevailing conditions. And, Life, being always dynamic, determines both the condition and the resulting manifestation.

This inner clarity gave me the explanation to the earlier query which commenced with comparing the moss with the conifer and then comparing other manifestations of Life, also.

The resulting insight produced a welcome certitude because I had realized an important link for my understanding of Life in action.

17

The Flowing Stream

This stream, I had believed, was well known to me. I was acquainted with its location, its sounds, its coolness, the riparian vegetation, the rocks that influence the flow, and with many of the species of creatures that live in the water and on its banks.

Yet, as I stood on the footbridge, that day, taking in this peaceful scene, I comprehended that the stream I saw was not, at all, the one that I had seen even just a moment earlier. Furthermore, it would never, ever, again be the same.

I had been well aware that the stream was affected by such change-producing factors as oxygenation, climate and organic and inorganic elements. Now, I perceived all this as part of indivisible Life.

After dwelling a while to enjoy the stream, I proceeded back to the car. On the way, I passed through a lush meadow filled with California poppies and scurrying ground squirrels.

Surveying the landscape around me, I thought about the stream I had just visited, and the grass, the poppies, the ground squirrels, and I sharing Life's pattern of continuous change.

18

Of Clouds
and Sycamores

It was a day that provided a wonderful opportunity to watch the clouds in the sky.

As the dense clouds billowed over the mountain range, which separates the valley from the ocean, I could see that they were heavily laden with moisture picked up over the water.

Driven by the wind, the cloud mass scattered upon reaching the middle of the valley.

Now, it was comparatively easy to distinguish one cloud from another. In fact, one could tell them apart by their shape, size, color, speed, and location.

Subsequent to dispersion, the clouds merged again and thereby lost their individuality. It was, therefore, only for a fleeting moment that the clouds appeared as individual. In the ongoing cycle, the ocean's moisture carried by the clouds would return again to earth.

Looking from sky to ground, I noticed the previous years' large sycamore leaves decaying and becoming one with the ground below the trees. On the branches, buds were ready to open leaves to a new season.

I recognized in the clouds and sycamores the common strand of Life's ongoingness.

19

Musings
in the Rain

As I was walking along the lake, I observed the intricate pattern which the rain made on the water. Each individual drop created ever-widening circles. These concentric circles resulted in a vivid, temporary, interlocking design covering the entire lake.

I could not help but wonder about the origin of the rain drops. How far had they traveled? And what had they previously experienced as water? What was their future? In what cells would they periodically be active? It was fascinating to consider the life of raindrops from a global perspective.

I passed the lake, and proceeded on the trail into the adjacent wooded area. One particular location on the trail was quite wet. On the edge of this muddy spot I noticed an earthworm about four inches in length. It appeared to be just an ordinary worm such as I had seen many times before in inclement weather. However, on that occasion I discovered something about earthworm behavior and personality.

As the worm reached the spot where I was standing, a movement on my part seemed to im-mediately signal something to it. Instinctively, it reared up half its length in a defensive stance.

Instantly, the worm was transformed into a miniature, cobra-like, creature. After pausing about three seconds, it backed up and went very rapidly in reverse until it, evidently, felt secure. It then resumed its normal way of crawling.

It was obvious that the earthworm possessed its share of Life's all-inclusive, self-protective intelligence.

Further along the trail I came upon a clearing bordered by a lush vegetation of wild blackberries, thimbleberries, and mint.

The rain, by then, had slowed down to the point that raindrops fell only sporadically. I could feel a drop bouncing off my ear, then others off the tip of my nose, my shoulders, and the top of my head. My nerves were completely tuned in to the rhythm of the droplets landing.

It was then that I looked carefully at the vegetation in front of me, and was spellbound by what I saw.

As each raindrop met a leaf, the leaf would move ever so gently. However, since there were so many leaves, there was continuing rain-inspired leaf motion. I felt privileged to witness this wonderful, magical scene of movement.

While watching the rain and leaves interacting,

I, myself, was still feeling the drops intermittently landing on various parts of my body.

Sharing this experience with the leaves, I felt closely connected with them. I knew, intuitively, that the plants must also sense each individual raindrop as it touched and slid off. And as the rain reached the plants' roots they would react to this Life giving moisture.

At that moment in time, I was conscious of the plants' sensations and my own being in harmony.

20

The Apple and the Food Chain

"An apple a day" is a maxim that I have tried to follow, whenever possible. I must have eaten a lot of apples in my lifetime. They were juicy, dry, sweet, tart, small, large, red, yellow, green and variegated.

Usually, I would also take one along when going on a hike, as I did on that day.

Having walked steadily for quite a while, I elected to rest a bit by sitting on an old log in the shade of a maple tree. A good time to eat my apple, I thought.

Something made me contemplate the apple as I had never done before. This took my mind, by visualization, on an extended journey. It all started with some questions.

What is the intelligence that makes my body convert the elements of the apple into living cells?

And how do the elements of the apple understand to act and react with the cells of my body in order to nourish and be of benefit?

And, similarly, what is the intelligent interaction between everything else in the food chain?

Well, my sojourn on that log took a lot longer than I had anticipated.

That day, the apple proved to be not only food for the body, but also considerable food for thought.

I pondered, intensely, on why every cell and element is aware of what to do.

The answer was eventually clear to me—it was a confirmation of the oneness of Life.

I comprehended that the apple and my body, and the entire food chain, are manifestations of the one Life. I recognized the apple in my hand to be the consequence of Life's perpetual interaction. And, furthermore, I recognized that as the cells of this apple meet the cells of my body, and as the cells and elements of the entire food chain meet, this perpetual interactive rhythm of Life continues.

With this insight, I appreciated my apple more than ever.

21

Seeing Life's Perpetual Progression

Across the cove from where I was standing, the waves were pounding against the base of "Sea Lion Rock." The sea lions, however, seemed entirely unperturbed by the ocean's action. I could see that some were, in fact, dozing.

On my side of the cove, I, too, was relaxed at the edge of a cypress grove. I marveled at the determination with which the trees clung to this rocky and windy part of the Pacific Coast.

Besides the cypress trees, the vegetation was predominantly blue-flowered California wild lilac, grey-foliaged California sagebrush, and pale orange sticky monkey flowers.

This was the setting which I admired when I saw Life in a compressed panorama.

It so happened that I observed three cypress trees at once.

The first was a vigorous and mature specimen, about thirty-five feet in height. Not far away, under its canopy, was a thriving six inch tall seedling. And, approximately fifteen feet away, there was an old cypress tree entirely devoid of any foliage—its skeleton bleached grey by sun and storms.

My first, and immediate, impulse was to label the third tree as "dead." But I hesitated.

I recognized in these three trees, as well as in

the ocean and in the sea lions, the indivisible oneness of Life in continuity.

The ancestor tree, long ago, had passed Life on to the now mature tree, and it, in turn, to the seedling.

All three trees during their presence in this spot absorbed and transpired vital moisture. Some of this water became a component of the ocean. And evaporation is continuing and repeating the process.

Generations of sea lions and generations of cypress trees participated in the interaction that goes on, globally, to provide carbon dioxide and oxygen.

And what is the real condition of the skeleton tree now? It could hardly be called "dead." This cypress, too, is still very much in Life's flow through its progeny and it will supply essential nutrients to future generations.

Indeed, this tree, though transformed from its

earlier appearance, continues to be a part of the interminable cycle of Life.

What a privilege it was seeing Life in progressive perpetuity.

22

A Journey to the Ancient Bristlecone Pine Forest

Subsequent to spending a few marvelous days in magnificent, breathtakingly beautiful, Yosemite Valley, surrounded by waterfalls (the highest dropping a combined total of approx. 2,425 feet), streams, meadows, wildflowers, and glacier-polished granite, I headed for INYO National Forest in the White Mountains high country.

I wanted to personally see and commune with the oldest known living things on earth, Pinus longaeva—the ancient bristlecone pines.

Rhododendrons (azaleas) and dogwoods were in different stages of bloom as I drove from the Valley's approximately 4000 feet elevation to Tioga Pass at about 9,000 feet.

The air on Tioga Pass was cool and crisp. And remnants of the winter's snow could still be seen, especially on the large subalpine Tuolomne Meadows.

I passed pristine Tenaya Lake which I knew from previous excursions. I would swim here, again, on my way back. For now, I wanted to continue.

The next large body of water that I saw on my route was Mono Lake, with its grotesquely-shaped mineral deposits, as high as fifteen feet and above. These "Tufa," as they are called, make this a fascinating place, indeed; one that I had also explored several years earlier.

A short drive from Mono Lake was the Devil's

Postpile National Monument. It is a very unusual geological formation of basaltic columns protruding sixty feet out of the mountainous terrain, about 7,600 feet above sea level.

Not far from there, I also saw a lot of obsidian, a black volcanic glass-like rock used by the early Indians to make into arrowheads.

I had been driving again for a while, when I stopped at a natural hot spring to break for lunch.

This was a delightful spot. A cold running stream with an extremely hot spring bubbling up, from deep within the earth, in its center.

My lunch would be sliced cucumber and hot beans.

In preparation for the lunch dish, I placed a can of beans in the hottest part of the spring, after puncturing the lid to allow the steam to escape.

No time was lost in getting myself into the stream and moving from hot to cold and back, all the while enjoying the temperature variations available to me.

The ambient air was still chilly, but I was leisurely comfortable in the water as I waited for my lunch entree to heat up. When it was ready, I dressed warmly and settled down to what tasted like an exquisite gourmet meal.

I could not have asked for more. I felt serene and at peace in this little Shangri-La with Life all around me.

Staying as long as I could, I finally packed my stuff and resumed the trip to my destination.

The last segment of my journey was through an area of sparse vegetation. This was due to very little annual precipitation at this elevation of about 10,000 feet.

And then I saw them—the ancient bristlecone pines in all of their picturesque glory. The oldest one is estimated to be over four thousand years of age and still producing viable seeds. Between ten and thirty feet in height, they were gnarled and twisted. Annually, they endured storms, drought, and the lack of topsoil.

Tenaciously growing in weathered limestone, these venerable trees, shaped by the severe elements of this remote location, were absolutely awe-inspiring.

I was almost mesmerized by the fact that some of these trees were flourishing saplings at the time of ancient Egypt.

The bristlecone pines share their abode with mountain chickadees, golden-mantled ground squirrels, and various other creatures. That day, I joined them because I wanted to learn something from these ancient trees.

As I sat there in this quiet place, I felt deeply conscious of the one Life of which we were all manifestations.

These survivors of long ago, these four-thousand-year-olds, were now also my contemporaries.

Here, we were, the bristlecone pines, the chickadees, the squirrels, and I, all living and breathing, one precious moment at a time.

At that very instant we were silently linked by Life.

My visit with the ancient bristlecone pines has helped me to comprehend that everything occurs in the ever-present now. Even four thousand years was always lived, and experienced, just one moment at a time.

23

Realizing Connectedness Everywhere

Traveling is something that I enjoy immensely. Examples of the many highlights that readily come to mind are:

Visiting the Grand Canyon, Yosemite Valley, the High Sierra, Yellowstone, the Grand Tetons, the Virgin Islands, desert oases, Big Sur and Point Lobos, and the historic and cultural sites of our nation's capital.

Climbing the Alps, and visiting cathedrals, castles, and museums of Europe.

Cruising the river Nile, and seeing the pyramids, temples, and tombs of Egypt.

Riding on horseback, through a narrow opening in the cliffs, to reach the ancient city of Petra in Jordan.

Seeing the volcanic peaks, the colorful vegetation, and the coral-rimmed lagoons of Polynesia.

Tramping through the verdant jungles of the Americas, and visiting the pyramids of the ancient Maya civilization.

Seeing the temples, shrines, gardens, and castles in Japan.

Crossing the Yangtze and Volga rivers in China and Russia, respectively, and touring places of cultural and scenic interest.

Visiting numerous focal points of nature and culture in Bali, Malaysia, and Thailand.

Hiking through the lush rainforest of Costa Rica, and seeing a profusion of vegetation and species of all kinds.

Visiting Jerusalem and the shrines of the Holy Land, and being at the Sea of Galilee at sunrise.

The differences and contrasts in people, geography, religion, culture, habitations, and flora and fauna of the places visited are considerable and numerous. However, it is these very differences and contrasts that make living a rich and rewarding adventure.

Because of my recognition that all I saw was the manifestation of the one Life, I always realized complete connectedness in the many locales and environments.

24

Awareness

eflecting on the manifold experiences cited, I recognize that they contributed significantly to my deep, and abiding awareness that

All Is One Life—the One Divine Life.

About the Author

Bert Gerlitz retired after a public service career, spanning more than thirty years, in which he held positions as Superintendent of Parks, Fine Arts Director, and Chief of Protocol. As Chief of Protocol, Mr. Gerlitz had the unique opportunity to frequently meet and work with people of many countries of the world.

Mr. Gerlitz holds a Master of Arts in Political Science and a B.A. in Recreation. He also has extensive background in horticulture.

The author and his wife, Ursula, have been married over forty years. They have two children and six grandchildren. Ursula, a former ballerina in Europe, was for thirty years director of her own ballet school in the U.S.

One of his avocations, which he and his wife have shared over the years, has been traveling. He has visited more than twenty-nine countries, observing the prevailing life and culture.

He considers every facet of his life including youth, education, career, and retirement, an ongoing process of learning and maturation.

The author has always loved nature—the great outdoors—for the recreation, profound inspiration, and illumination to be gained.

All Is One Life reflects the enlightenment and insights realized by the author's frequent communion with nature.

The author's philosophy encompasses a firm awareness that the oneness of Life is basic to existence.